BRITAIN
This Beautiful Land

Dedicated to
Douglas and Jack

First English edition published by
    Colour Library International Ltd.
© 1983 Illustrations and Text:
    Colour Library International Ltd.
    99 Park Avenue, New York, N.Y. 10016, U.S.A.
This edition is published by Crescent Books
Distributed by Crown Publishers, Inc.
h g f e d c b a
Colour separations by FER-CROM,
    Barcelona, Spain.
Display and text filmsetting
    by ACESETTERS LTD., Richmond, Surrey, England.
Printed and bound in Barcelona,
    Spain by Cayfosa and Eurobinder.

Library of Congress Catalog Card Number: 83-70123

CRESCENT 1983

Dep. Leg. B. 13.132/83

BRITAIN
This Beautiful Land

Written and Designed by
PHILIP CLUCAS MSIAD

Produced by
Ted Smart and David Gibbon

CRESCENT BOOKS

No country in the world is richer than Britain in its patchwork of natural beauty. It is a mélange formed by the play of light and shade upon the landscape, by the tones which moss, lichen and fern impart upon mellow stonework, by the placing of spired church or ruined castle within the scene, and by the memories that have been stitched into the fabric of her landscape – into thyme-scented downland and primrose-haunted hedgerow; into silver threads of stream and darkling reed-mere.

The landscape of England, Scotland and Wales is one of rich and subtle contrast, where variety is the key to abiding fascination, and upon which each season paints its own freshness – be it the sight of wind-racked elms beyond a cornfield, poppy-studded amid the harvest gold, and shimmering in a summer's haze; the smell of wild hops hanging thickly from autumn bine; a grey winter's landscape, grizzled by sleet, its chill solitude broken only by the harsh call of the crows; or by the first flush of springtide, whose yearly appearance seems to exude the very essence of pastoral verse –

> *When weeds, in wheels, shoot long and lovely and lush;*
> *Thrush's eggs look little low heavens, and thrush*
> *Through the echoing timber does so rinse and wring*
> *The ear, it strikes like lightnings to hear him sing;*
> *The glassy peartree leaves and blooms, they brush*
> *The descending blue; that blue is all in a rush*
> *With richness; the racing lambs too have fair their fling.*

With variety goes surprise. Britain is a country of happy surprises, and there is no need to travel far to be pleasantly astonished. In the West, among rounded hills and soft yielding pasture, one suddenly arrives at the bleak tablelands of Dartmoor and Exmoor; and at Glastonbury there is an unexpected extent of fen whose flatness seems to suggest the landscape of Cambridgeshire. The long green walls of the South and North Downs – with their far-reaching views over the oast-houses, hop fields and orchards of Kent – are equally joyful surprises: the Weald is another of them. East Anglia has a kind of rough heath country of its own, that one never expects to find there, but is always delighted to see. After the easy rolling meadows of the Shires, the dramatic Peak District with its steep scarp never fails to astonish, for it seems to have no business there. Similarly, to the north, there are remnants of the Ice Age in the flowers and shrubs of Teesdale – alpine gentians and juniper – whilst a short distance away drifts of bluebells, wood anemones and wild garlic carpet the primeval woodlands that crowd the vales.

Another characteristic of the British landscape is its exquisite moderation – born of a compromise between wildness and tameness. Here the hand of nature and the works of man harmonize: the hedges, the wooden fences, even the low stone walls that bind the northern fells, all have been gently subdued by nature until at last they might have been natural growths themselves, like the mosses that cover their wood and stone. Indeed, man has no need to be ashamed of the extent of his handiwork – where in Devon he built his thatched cottages of colour-wash cob, where in Herefordshire he used his timber and plaster to such striking 'magpie-like' effect, or where in the grim north he built his grey peel towers as defence against raiders from across the border. It is no accident either that the works of our earliest ancestors – such as the tall stones of Callernish, the 'Druids' Circle at Keswick, or any mighty prehistoric earthwork like Maiden Castle or Uffington Hill Fort – stand in surroundings of peerless loveliness. Thus are built (at a later age) the Abbey of Tintern on the Wye, Dryburgh in the arm of the Tweed, Rievaulx in the green cup of the Hambledon Hills, and Fountains Abbey nestled amongst trees and rocks. Of similar merit are Durham Cathedral set high on its rock promontory overhanging the Wear, Lincoln overlooking half a county, and Ely poised triumphantly above the Fens. Nor was this sense of beauty lost with the first flush of enthusiasm – that material prosperity did not blunt the medieval mind can be seen at a glance around any Cotswold village, where houses have an irregularity and colouring that make them fit snugly into the landscape as though they were as much a piece of natural history as the trees that shade them. Such landscapes are a comfort to man, yet the countryside has not relinquished all of its ancient savagery and power – the vast moors, the mountains and the cruel seascapes still hold him in awe.

The enormous variety of countryside to be found in Britain is what makes a journey through its landscape so infinitely rewarding. In the succeeding chapters this progression is charted, and encompasses all the regions of these enchanted Isles – from the magnificently divergent landscape of the Western shores, through the chalk downlands of Southern England, to the lush pasture and ploughland of East Anglia and the Fens. It journeys to the Cotswolds and Malvern Hills, to the gentle terrain of the vales and the Welsh borderlands, and into the remote fastnesses of the mountains of Wales. From the Shire country of England's heartland the warmth of the South is supplanted by the rugged grandeur of Lakeland, and the cold fells and sheltered dales of the North. The final chapters cross the Cheviots and the Roman Wall to the marcherlands and Southern uplands of Scotland, which in turn melt into the full glorious fury of the Highlands, whose dramatic scenery of remote mountains, lochs and islands are the equal of any.

The West Country
Land of Contrast and Rich Diversity

It is pleasant to think of the West Country – with its long coastline abutting the surging swell of two seas and the crashing breakers of the open ocean – as though it were a country in itself. Indeed, there is a sense in which it was always so, for since man first roamed these Isles the Plain of Somerset, with its all but impenetrable landscape of marsh and lagoon, has formed a barrier between the lands of Devon and Cornwall and the rest of England. Early lines of communication consisted of tortuous trackways which always followed the highest contour to avoid the steep fall of streams and the area's tidal estuaries. The trails through Somerset and Dorset, where they were low lying or progressed through forest, were virtually impassable; in some parts of these counties this remained true right up to the advent of the railways. Thus was born the West Countryman's close affinity with the wild waters of his native coastline (sea-voyage was less fraught with hazard than overland travel) forging that proud kinship with the sea that in Elizabethan times controlled the destiny of the English Realm.

Cornwall, Devon and Somerset are traditionally set apart from the bulk of England, yet these Lands of the West possess the widest diversity of scenery to be found anywhere in Britain – even within their own individual county borders. Thus are the broad, sweeping moorlands of Dartmoor, with its tors and denuded high rocks, contrasted by the mild estuaries of East Devon so close at hand. Similarly, the grandeur of Bodmin Moor to the West in Cornwall and the harsh granite cliffs of the sea-coast are the direct antipathy of the gentle 'lost' worlds where birds flash in the leaf-canopied sunlight of lanes that rise but half a mile from shore or mere: here lies the West Country's true beauty – a beauty of informality, of secret places where sweet violets, primroses, wild garlic and flowers without number mingle with moss and damp-scented fern: where lichen-covered trees grow in woodlands haunted by stonechat, and apple trees long abandoned to nature stoop heavily under the weight of autumn fruit. Such joys are largely a matter of glimpse and chance – always of the hidden byway – and unknown to strange eyes.

The variety of the Western Landscape is due, as it is everywhere, to the geological variety of its composition. The old red sandstone of northern Exmoor, with its rolling expanse of heath and bracken given over to centuries of wind and rain; or Dartmoor, with its peat-coloured streams that criss-cross the moor, creating areas of swamp – intensely green, yet very dangerous – bear an entirely different vegetation from the upper greensand of the Somerset Heights. These sweep down in silhouette against the southern sky to enclose wooded orchards and pastures: here the upland ash and the rhododendron flourish in profusion, and willows shed their characteristic melancholy onto the scene. It is a land of fertile alluvial plain – dotted with black-faced sheep, and ponies (the lineal descendants of the Anglo-Saxon 'wild horse') –

through which silver rivers flow quietly onward to the broad surges of the bar and the everlasting thunder of the long Atlantic swell.

Somerset is perhaps the most varied county of all. Nothing could be more perfect in contrast than the shaven slopes and lustrine cliffs of the Mendips and the rugged contours of the Bredon Hills and Exmoor – with its rounded heather knolls, the deep blue of its waters and the green woods above, where in April and early May chaffinches, wrens and willow warblers sing in coppice woodland lush with campion and royal fern. From the south of the county the frowning heights of Blackdown look straight across Taunton Dene to the gently swelling Quantocks – filled with the soul of Coleridge and Wordsworth – and the little hills of Polden which lie below Glastonbury and the marshes of Brue.

These marshlands, now reclaimed and fertile, tell their own story of the days when Athelney and Glastonbury Tor were still islands, and when ships sailed right up the Parrett River. These lands of Alfred's exile – during Wessex' lowest fortune – have a singular dark beauty of their own, which, like the beauty of the Fens, is largely one of cloud and sky – yet the black soil and crimson osier withes give them a sinister colour – bringing back memories of Monmouth and his ill-starred confederates as though the blood of armies still stained the earth.

Of an age older than Alfred – older even than Arthur and his sword Excalibur (which is said to rest in Dozmary Pool) – is Glastonbury, which sheds the light of its legends over the surrounding marshlands. It should not be forgotten that this first Christian Church in Britain was never destroyed by the heathen invader, and that the traditions of Glastonbury stretch back to the childhood of Christ Himself; that William Blake, when he asked:

> *'And did those feet in ancient time,*
> *Walk upon England's mountains green?*
> *And was the Holy Lamb of God*
> *On England's pleasant pastures seen?*
> *And did the Countenance Divine*
> *Shine forth upon our clouded hills?'*

was referring to the green Mendip Hills. Here also, according to lore, Joseph of Arimathea journeyed to the pastures of Somerset, burying the Chalice of the Last Supper – the Holy Grail – under a spring on Glastonbury Tor.

In the West Country masons had at hand everything they needed in the nature of building stone. They followed the lead of those who built so faithfully at the Abbey of Glastonbury; and all the traditional changes in architectural style – from Saxon and Norman to Perpendicular style – can be followed in the Parish churches of Devon, Cornwall and Somerset. The High Gothic predominates, and many of the tallest church towers are likened to *'cold jewels set in a blaze of aquamarine that is the summer sky'.* Such are Episcopi with its deep Norman porch, whose sandstone has been burnt red by fire; the magnificently proportioned tower of Evercrech, and the proud churches of Chewton, Mendip and Wrington.

Chalk Country
The Downland Plain and the Chilterns

No matter where you wander in the Chalk Country of Southern England you will be on the downs, or on the edge of them. The Chiltern Hills range in a south-westerly direction from Bedfordshire, through Hertfordshire and Buckinghamshire to end in Oxfordshire. Immediately across the valley of the grey-ribboned Thames the Berkshire Downs connect the Chilterns on the east with the Marlborough Downs to the west – a land of vague mists and rooks cawing above the plough. From here they run southerly to Salisbury Plain – with only the smiling valley of the Pewsey Vale to break their rolling majestic range – from where they tumble in serried ridges into Dorset. There is a spacious permanence about this undulating landscape, where fields of feathered barley and pale green waving wheat are interspersed by great swathes of beech-riven chalk upland, pierced only occasionally by tracts of thorn-break and briar.

It is a land of bright harvest-sunshine and magnificent cloud formations. In summer it is shrouded in the rich blue of that *'unattainable flower of the sky'*, yet even on the most sultry of days there is always a breeze; and to lie on the springy turf and listen to the rustle the wind makes in the bennet is to imagine that you are hearing the whisper of some far-distant sea-tide. Even when frost holds the land there is still a breeze, but so slight that all is hushed and motionless, save for the hawk that hovers and side-slips and hovers again against a slate-grey sky as it searches for prey. On such winter days as these, clouds scurry across the scene, with here and there a gleam of sunlight to flame a blackened hedgerow amber for a moment and then pass onward to where the sun picks out the tower of a church in silver, or the gabled end of a brick-built cottage in military scarlet. Light and shadow everywhere change and exchange upon the lower chalk slopes of the hills, the evanescent sunshine clarifying small fields without number, whilst into this peace steals the sound of church-bells from distant downland hamlets.

The Chalkland valleys south of Salisbury Plain are rarely more than two miles wide, and nestling in their snug folds are trees of wych-elm and oak among glades of rowan and crab apple. Ash, hazel, hawthorne and sloe stand so thickly in wayside hedges that villages are often almost hidden from sight. Valley floors are a rich alluvial deposit from which the downs rise upwards on either side, supplanting pasture for ploughland as the soils become thinner and the white chalk breaks through. Among the water-meads of the combe, rivulets promote the growth of withy-alder and a carpet of lush green grass (where moorhens make their nests) is spangled and starred in the first freshness of the year by innumerable wild flowers. They come to the very edge of the chalk stream – the little bluebell-like campanula, the squinancywort, the yellow bedstraw, the delicate purple scabious, the lilac-coloured rampion and the creamy-white butterfly orchis.

Topping the scarp of the chalkland district are monuments which point to the vast antiquity of human settlement within this hill-country – an area once the centre of a religion now lost to the knowledge of man. We can only speculate as to the motivating factors which prompted the raising of such incredible monuments as Avebury, Stonehenge and the awesome magnitude of the man-made mound of Silbury Hill. Less spectacular, though no less impressive, works abound in this open countryside – grey wethers and sarsens, dolmen and megaliths stand in fields and on bare downs like human figures frozen for all time, marking the route to Wiltshire's Neolithic cathedrals. From a later era the White Horse of Uffington on the sweeping Berkshire chalk points to the deification of Epona by Iron-Age Celts who cut her sinuous form into the grassy hillside in the centuries predating Christ, when the period of the horse cult first became prominent.

Of a considerably earlier age are the hills themselves; formed during the Cretaceous period. However, unlike the chalkland of Wiltshire and Berkshire, the Chilterns are never referred to as 'downs.' They display much of the downland character but cling to their own rigid identity, the signature of which are their beechwoods – dense, silent places (as only the high woods of the Chilterns can be silent), embowered in 'Gothic' avenues of leaf, branch and sinewed trunk – bathed in the opalescent light invariably associated with the area. In springtime the Chilterns are a sea of bluebells and cherry blossom, and in early summer nightingales may be heard: always there is the smell of beech leaves and cherry wood, and the curl of smoke ascending through trees – the blue smoke of wood fires.

The South East
Weald and Chalk Downland

There is nothing spectacular, there is neither the grandeur of mountains nor the sweep of great rivers to add drama to the aspect of South-East England. It is a land of tranquil beauties; of rolling chalk downland, areas of pine and broad-leaved woodland, greensand hills rich with vegetation, little streams in wooded valleys and agricultural land of many shades – of plough, pasture and orchard. The landscape displays a harmony that is at once varied and homely – almost intimate – and peculiarly English.

The area's many different geological formations compound its diversity and have effect upon both the flora and fauna as well as the distinctive building styles of this south-eastern corner of England. Not the least of its treasures are to be found in architectural features – in the little Saxon and Romanesque churches faced with chalk, tufa and split flint; in the ragstone castles of England's defensive shore, now tinged with the colour of honey by time-encrusted lichens; in Kent's cylindrical oast-houses with their red-slated roofs and wooden wind cowls, used for drying hops; in the whitewashed clapboarding of Tudor farmhouses; and in the mellow timber and brick of 18th century village cottages.

To treat such a varied tract as the four counties of Kent, Sussex, Surrey and Hampshire as one unit is not an easy task, yet all have at least two features in common, which are in fact the South-East's predominant characteristic. Firstly, there are the chalk downlands, the most significant range of southern hills which include the South Downs of Sussex and the long line of the North Downs which rise in Hampshire and traverse Surrey and Kent to end abruptly at Shakespeare's Cliff near Folkestone. These uplands, dappled in spring and summer with moving blue shadow, are bare of foliage where the chalk comes near to the surface, but trees grow in profusion wherever pockets of clay supplant the chalk. Here beech trees predominate, forming clumps, that – like the Chanctonbury Ring and the thickets at Cranborne Chase – are far-seen landmarks invariably cast into prominence by great billowing crowns of shining cloud.

Much of these rolling hills remains unwooded, yet there is compensation in the beauty of springy turf scattered with hairbells and tiny heathers, and spiced with marjoram and wild thyme. It is in remote places such as these – on the wind-swept ridges of South-East England – that plovers wheel above clover-scented turf cropped since time immemorial by great flocks of sheep which find pasture in the downland sheep-walks. Near their summit are trackways worn into existence by the tread of Neolithic man; and along these ancient paths are to be found dolmens, stone circles, flint workings and haunting human imagery – chalk figures incised in the turf – such as the Long Man of Wilmington and the Cerne Abbas Giant – relics of an age when Salisbury Plain was the centre of a civilization which flourished more than four thousand years ago. The very remoteness of such mysterious hill-top places attracted superstition, and local lore states that Woden, one-eyed and wise beyond all knowing, stalks the lonely downs wildly hunting on black and stormy nights for the lost souls of his ancient peoples.

Stretching between the steep escarpment of the North and South Downs lies the area's second notable feature, a wonderful expanse of woodland – much of it a relic of the great British forest of *Andred* – which comprises the Weald of Southern England. Its timber has been stripped for shipbuilding – the navy's *Hearts of Oak* – and for use in the numerous ironworks of Sussex and lowland Kent, evidence of which can be seen in the old hammer ponds which dot the landscape. Surviving areas of the *Andred* tend to be small in extent and consist of ash, hazel, chestnut and the ever-present oak, but what these woodlands lack in scale is more than made up for by their intimate charm – by small brooks that meander through them, and by the carpet of primroses, bluebells and delightful 'wind flowers' (the wood anemone) which yearly show their blooms among the gnarled roots of great trees, struggling through briar growth and blackthorn to herald the advent of spring.

Always there are the Downs on one hand and the fertile expanse of wooded valley on the other, stretching away as far as the eye can see. In summer there is a brilliant colouring in farmland, nestling as it does beneath the chalk uplands and shielded by discreet pockets of coppice woodland. Here the rich tint of poppies growing on the margin of ploughland, in the field hedge, and on the downs themselves bring a splash of scarlet to set off the viridian of distant hills and the flaming-gold of ripening harvest. Indeed, among this lush landscape of abundance with its orchards and pastures, nature seems to speak with the very voice of scripture –

Thou visitest the earth, and waterest it:
Thou greatly enrichest it with the river of God,
Which is full of water: thou preparest them corn,
When thou had so provided for it.
Thou waterest the ridges thereof abundantly:
Thou settlest the furrows thereof:
Thou makest it soft with showers:
Thou blessest the springing thereof.
Thou crownest the year with thy goodness;
And thy paths drop fatness.
They drop upon the pastures of the wilderness:
And the little hills rejoice on every side.
The pastures are clothed with flocks:
The valleys also are covered over with corn:
They shout for joy, they also sing.

The Eastern Counties
The Broads, Brecklands and the Fens

The landscape of East Anglia is typically one of sweeping views, in low relief but by no means flat. It comprises areas of intense contrast: of Fenland, whose dark waters cowl sedge-swamps and reed-beds in shadowed morasses and lagoons; of estuary, mile upon mile of mud flats, and 'meals' – vast salt marshes – a lonely kingdom of wildfowl where wading birds and geese flock in their thousands. The landscape also encompasses the curious peat-dug Broadland where bitterns boom their eerie call – a labyrinth of dykes and half-reclaimed marshes – impenetrable to any but a native; and sandy heath known as Breckland whose abiding primeval spirit is reflected in the gloomy flint-pits of Grime's Graves, quarried locally four thousand years ago. Such features are among the least spoilt of any in Britain, and are experienced to the full in wintertime, when blackened heaths and mist-haunted reed-meres reveal the solitary nature of a land racked by piercing winds driven from the North Sea.

In direct contrast to these desolate spots, the majority of the eastern counties is given over to intensive arable farmland, whose rich dark soils are numbered among the most fertile in the world. Here the landscape is entirely pastural, swelling into gentle golden ridges, the crests of which carry hedgerows, the occasional coppice and farmsteads. This lush countryside of stream-splashed water meadows and fresh valleys has a character very much its own. It is this enchanting aspect of landscape that held one of its most famous sons in awe. For John Constable the calm of his native East Anglia held a particular fascination, *'the beauty of the surrounding scenery,'* he wrote, *'its gentle declivities, the luxuriant meadow flats sprinkled with flocks and herds, its well-cultivated uplands, its woods and rivers with numerous scattered villages and churches, farms and picturesque cottages, all impart to this particular part an elegance hardly anywhere else to be found.'* If 'elegance' has perhaps changed its implication, the scene has altered little since Constable first painted it, and the Stour Valley still expresses, perhaps as completely as anywhere, the spirit of pastoral England at its best.

As with Constable's Suffolk canvases, it is the element of air and towering columns of cloud – an effect heightened by an intense vibration of light created both by the nearness of the sea, and the spread of inland waters – that combine to characterise the unique quality of the East Anglian scene. Contrasting regions as diverse as Fenland and Breck, pasture and Broad, are united under the all-embracing skyscapes of the eastern counties, and each, however different from its neighbour, is evoked by that vista of open, long horizons where heaven and lonely earth seem to mingle and melt into a fusion of misty blue distance.

Throughout East Anglia water dominates the landscape – be it in the mixture of saltings, shingle ridges, sand dunes and marsh of the Norfolk coastline; or the sluggish rivers (some rising only a mile or two from the sea) which form reed-choked meres varying in nature from secluded lakelets to vast expanses, as wide as inland seas; or the fragmented marshes of the Broads, scented with meadow sweet and the sharp tang of water mint. The inconsistencies of tides have silted over harbour mouths, such as Cley, that once dispatched whalers to Iceland, and ships against the Armada. Nowhere, however, does the influence of water prevail and impose itself more upon the landscape than in the Fen country of Cambridgeshire and Lincolnshire, where a million acres of rich agricultural land have been claimed by the drainage of Fenland rivers – the Great Ouse, the Nene, the Wissey and the Welland. Here, almost treeless fields are endlessly intersected by runnels which, although artificial, are in many ways one of the most distinctive features of the landscape. Fenland is a vast flat region – much of it below sea-level – upon which bad weather can induce a depression unprecedented in other surroundings, and the winter's bleakness must be experienced through long months to be realised. Yet, for all this, the Fens possess an abiding beauty – not borne of the careless English adornment of hill, stream and meadow, but one in which wide spaces and vast restless skyscapes alter its features with each variation of weather, and demand a tribute to each changing mood.

Fenland, more than other regions, is naturally bound up with its own history. In its original state the area was an overgrown, waterlogged morass – in winter an inland sea, and in summer a swamp of stagnant meres, teeming with fish and fowl. Its few inhabitants lived on the remote patches of firm ground that stood out like islands above a clouded sea: little wonder, therefore, that this traditional haunt of lost causes should attract the sterner monastic Orders to these remote island sites far removed from the turbulence of medieval life. Here they gradually transformed the fen into scattered settlements – green oases about their mighty churches. Such were Thorney, Ramsey, Chatteris and Crowland – whose shattered fragments of abbeys remain – yet greatest of all, in extent and importance, is the Isle of Ely, where the Norman Minster still stands out defiantly against the violet light of the endless flats of the Great Level – the medieval flower of the surrounding domain it had conquered.

The West Midland Vales
The Cotswolds and Malvern Hills

The rolling countryside of the West-Midland Vales – a landscape of elm-fringed water meadows of the Severn and Avon, and orchards laden with damson, cherry, apple and pear – is the green heartland of England. It is the misty-green vale from which Elgar drew his music and, centuries beforehand, Langland had his vision of Piers Plowman. At its centre is the Vale of Evesham, perhaps the most productive fruit-growing district in all Britain. The land is naturally at its most beautiful at Eastertide when its orchards are enveloped in a white foam of blossom: in pockets of wayside vegetation bluebells are found in such profusion that coppice-margins and hedgebanks are *'washed wet like lakes'* – bathed in pools of light – whose sheen continually changes as the drooping flower-heads swirl to heavily-scented breezes.

The quiet capital of its own vale, the town of Evesham arose round an abbey of which only the bell tower now survives. As with the landscape's other ecclesiastical glories, notably the medieval abbey at Tewkesbury and the cathedral towers of Gloucester and Worcester, form and construction have been meticulously honed to complement the surrounding countryside's unique qualities of light – an effect best observed (in the alliterative words of Langland's poetry), *'In somer season when soft is the sonne.'* Indeed, it is this element of luminosity – of gathering light – that best characterises the jagged Malvern Hills to the west, and illuminates the gentle, bow-headed, 'whale-back' landscape of the Cotswolds which stretch beyond the vale to south and to east.

It is here in the wold, with its predominance of honey-brown masonry, that the stones themselves appear to glow. When the limestone is first quarried it is a bleached grey, yet with the mellowing influence of time, cottages, barns and dry stone walling blush a tawny hue and acquire a radiance that marvellously merges the work of man with the spacious beauties of the surrounding hills. These are the elements that go to produce the Cotswold picture. It is a vision of undulating hillsides heaving buff-green into the distance, their thin fringes of scattered beech clear-cut against a crowded sky. It is the seclusion of valleys, lined with pollard willows, along which a clear brook threads its silver course – a haunt of lazy, dappled trout and gadding mayfly. It is a land of expansive pastures dotted with cowslip, orchis, celandine, scabious and buglewort; of hedgeside daisies; and fallow fields that sweep the brow of the wold and then fall to the vale below. There are few villages to be seen; only now and then in the distance comes a hamlet, caught in a fold of hills, whose gabled stone houses with weathered stone-slate roofs reflect the sun amongst the green of moss and the yellow of lichens.

Cotswold villages are invariably strung along the course of a stream: the Windrush, the Coln, or the Evenlode, to name but a few, and each displays a careful craftsmanship and sense of style that is the particular achievement of the district. The 'Cotswold style' has remained a constant expression of local materials and need; it had its birth towards the close of the 14th century; certainly by the 15th century it had reached a high degree of maturity – as expressed by buildings such as Icomb Manor and those in the High Street at Chipping Campden. However, it is the smaller manor houses at Owlpen, Upper Slaughter, Upper Swell and Snowhill that epitomise the dignified Cotswold expression of pride in local prosperity and achievement.

A word must also be said for the churches. It is remarkable how many of these remain the primitive little structures that were raised almost a thousand years ago when the manors of the wold were first parcelled out among the Norman Lords. Though externally some of them might well belong to any medieval epoch, several (most notably at Elkstone and Hampnett) can reveal perfect Romanesque interiors hardly touched by the hand of time. The beginnings of prosperity in the 13th century – when the Cotswolds were the heart of England's wool industry – is reflected in an Early English group as typical as any in the country; North Cerney and Duntisbourne being particularly attractive, with their saddleback towers. The glory of the district is, however, the later 'wool churches' that, collectively, remain as grand a memorial to the munificence of their merchant patrons as to the genius of the masons who evoked such splendours from the resources of locally quarried limestone. Fabrics such as the Northleach, Fairford, Cirencester, Campden and Winchcombe parish churches rank with any in the land for their beauty of craftsmanship.

The Welsh Borderland
The Marcher Hills and Valleys

The countryside of the Welsh Borderland is possessed of a power and impressiveness – and elegance of spirit – that rivals anything that the rest of Britain can offer. Here a variety of elements, of river and dell, of orchard and swelling pasture, of woodland and hedgerow-patterned fields, mingle in a tangled complex of steep valleys and hills to produce an ensemble of sweetness and beauty.

A rural peace reigns over this landscape which spreads upwards from valley floors to the curving crests of the ridge and then drops again through skirting woods to where little rills curl among their water-meads. Seasonal colouring is everywhere apparent; in the greens and russet of bracken, in the black and purple of heather, and in the rain-soaked verdure of bent and bilberry. On a windy day it is an invigorating experience to follow the turf tracks that run along the Marcher crests; looking westwards into the wind to view the darkened, bold moorland summits, and beyond them to the azure outline of more hills (pierced occasionally by splashes of purple ploughland) and yet more ridges, backed by the profiles of the Welsh peaks. In the opposite direction lies the almost limitless expanse of the Midland Plain, heaving mile upon mile into a far distant haze. It is a prospect beloved of John Masefield, who knew well its moods and subtleties,

"I have seen dawn and sunset on moor and windy hills
coming in solemn beauty . . ."

The Marcher region lies between the two great estuaries of Dee and Severn and extends southwards from Chester through the vale country of Cheshire and Shropshire (the hills and finger-ridges of the south part of that county), the tumbled plain of Herefordshire and the uplands of Monmouthshire and Dean. Along its line rise the high hills of Wales, massed in close formation – sometimes sending spurs into English soil, sometimes parting to admit green tongues of farmland into valleys threaded by swift rivers. There is a wild beauty in these vales, with their small, white, half-timbered farmhouses in magpie garb, and tumbled woods dwarfed by the austere sweeps of the heights above. Through this land from north to south the old Borderline wavers, often with an arbitrary parting of neighbouring hills, but still largely following the direction of the turf breastwork built in the 8th century by the Mercian, King Offa.

The Welsh Borderland is a landscape of contrast – upland, rock formations, mountains such as the Wrekin in the west, and rich dairy pastures and grasslands to the north. At Ludlow, for example, can be seen a complete English composition with all the traditional features of harvest cornfields and a predominance of stately trees – oak, fir and beech. In contrast, the Stiperstones are sharp and bare with tor-like outcrops of dark rock – the haunt of kestrel and raven – or beyond to the singularly graceful peak of Corndon Hill facing sheer across country to the hedge-patterned mass of the Long Mountain and the copious triple summit of the Breidden hills.

Apart from intrinsic beauty, the Welsh Marches hold a history steeped in romance. The memory of early struggles is handed down in mighty earth-fastnesses – Croft Ambrey, Wapley, Nordy Bank – and in the husks of ruined castles such as Wigmore, Clun, Ludlow and Hopton, which stand as mute witness to centuries of turmoil and violence that abated only after the Civil War.

The subjugation of Wales was a task too formidable for direct under-taking, even by the Normans, so it came about that the Borderlands were divided out amongst the more enterprising of their soldier-adventurers who were given *carte-blanche* to build themselves fortifications from which they could conquer the wild and scattered native population. The new rulers established themselves by force and existed in watchful defence within the confines of their so-called Lordship Marchers. Nevertheless, in the majority of cases their rule was equable so that before long townships and villages grew up beneath Norman keeps: such were Wigmore, Hay, Montgomery, Clun and scores more – quiet places nowadays that seem to belong to their past, half asleep in the shadows of their castle crags. Thus, through the great medieval upheavals – the crumbling of the Llewellyn Princes, the encroachment of Marcher fiefs, the campaigning of the Plantagenets, and the culminating tragedy of Owain Glyndŵr – has this wild and once remote landscape been transformed into a tract of some of the quietest and most lovely of Country Shires.

Wales *The Spirit and the Face*

Wales is an extraordinary mixture of the obvious and the recondite, a country of romantic legends and ruined castles, yet the overpowering spirit of the landscape is one of Gothic drama – a wild mountainous terrain of vast, indigo, cloud-misted distances, pervaded by the sound of sweet water and birdsong. Here is a depth of vision leading you into the centre of an almost untouchable world of clear light and exhilarating vista – a land where curlews flock in their thousands to feed upon damp moorland, their wild plaint, at first joyous and then of long despairing lament, seems to haunt Wales eternally.

In the days of the Princes, Wales was always regarded as three entities, the Northern Kingdom of Gwynedd, The Middle Kingdom of Powis, and the Southern Kingdom of Deheubarth. Powis was never a very strong power and seldom stood by its own might; nowadays it is only a vague historical memory. Not so, however, the other two. Wales is only a unified country in the mind of the idealist – in practice it is divided into North and South. The division is precise and occurs at the River Dovey; this point is a boundary not only of Welsh feeling – between the Anglicized lands of South Wales, and the spirit of Celtic individualism which has been the hallmark of the Northern lands since the 13th century – but scenery also, the sharp mountains of the Cambrian Range lying to the north of the Dovey, whilst smoother, less dramatic mountains spread southwards across the Deheubarth landscape.

In Southern Wales history delivered a hammerblow to Welsh nationhood by the gradual inroads made by Norman Marcher Lords who extended English conquest from the mouth of the Wye as far west as Pembrokeshire's Atlantic headland. Along this fief, part of which is still referred to as 'Little England beyond Wales', are found the ruins of the most impressive castles in Wales – Caerphilly. Manorbier, Carew, Chepstow and Llanstephan, with a host more on a lesser scale of grandeur. Everywhere along this feudal tract the Norman and English cultures dominate – fine stone houses were constructed; magnificent churches were raised; and towns on the old English plan were built.

As the south coast of Wales has its line of castles stretching from the Marches to the ocean boundary, so has the Welsh northern seaboard a string of impregnable fortresses at Conway, Beaumaris, Rhuddlan, Caernarvon and Harlech – but these are of quite a different order. The former were as much baronial mansions as fortresses, whilst the latter, built by King Edward I after his conquest of Wales, were just fortified barracks for royal troops. The countryside around these bastions showed no signs of a spread of English culture and remains today as Welsh in speech, feeling and lack of architectural impulse as it ever was.

Under the yoke of Plantagenet kings the flower of Celtic independence retreated into the fastness of the Snowdonia landscape – vast mountains, notched in places like battlemented towers, with high passes and craggy peaks – from where the spirit of Welsh freedom occasionally resurfaced in the guise of her hero princes – Llywelyn the Great, Llywelyn ap Gruffydd and Owain Glyndŵr. Some part of this essence of defiance seems to linger in these wild, northern mountains to haunt this highland of rock and heather where nothing appears to have altered since the Ice Age; all is embraced by silence, save for the bleat of lambs, the sudden flight of snipe, or the solitary call of the rare red kite – described by one native poet as *'the living flame of the sky.'* Here are great sweeping moorlands, rising to mountainous masses 2,000 feet or more in height and interspersed with marsh-flats ablaze with golden gorse flower. Views are wide and horizons far: the wind sweeps freely across the vastness, and the skylark and meadow pipit's song is lost to the breeze. However, soaring above all – dominating all – is the ethereal azure mass of Snowdon – the focus of bardic song and sentiment throughout the ages.

North Wales is a land composed almost entirely of ancient rock formations whose contorted form and denuded surfaces were produced by ice pressure millions of years ago. In the great mass of the northern Cambrian Range, Snowdon at 3,500 feet, Carnedd Dafydd at 3,426 feet, and Carnedd Llewelyn at 3,484 feet, are sister peaks – barren on their upper slopes and in winter season snow covered – their summits reflected in lonely blue and black lakes of crystal purity set high up in their mountain folds. South and East of Snowdon, on the 2,000 feet contour, are the Arenig moorlands, the Berwyn Mountains and the Harlech Dome. These, in turn, are skirted by a rolling landscape intersected by moor and patches of peat-mire, which are almost intimidating in their sense of splendid immunity from traces of human activity – all, that is, except for an occasional ruined stone and slate cottage, the long deserted shelter of shepherds seeking the high summer pastures.

The central plateau melts into Mid-Wales, and the Plynlimon group whose characteristics are rounded grassy shapes, worn into innumerable furrows, culminating in one very definite mountain – Plynlimon. Although in height it only rises 2,465 feet, there is something very grand and distinctive about it. Plynlimon represents the corner stone of all three provinces of Medieval Wales, and also, in the peat bogs of its slopes, gives birth to both the Severn and the Wye.

Further south, along the Cambrian backbone of Wales, lie the contorted hills, tall shadowy rock gorges and great cascades of foaming water that form the Brecon Beacons. They rise to 2,906 feet at Pen y Fan and are named from their use as sites for signal fires. The wind-lashed summits have a dragonlike outline, sporting sheer precipices which fall 600 feet and have been likened to the crests of giant waves about to break into the deep valley gorges, or *'cwns,'* below. On either side of the Beacons are the East and West Black Mountains. They have very distinctive individualities, and it is unfortunate and confusing that they should share a similar name – even the colour is wrong, for they are composed of outcrops of red Devonian sandstone. The Eastern group – marking the end of Wales, and the beginning of England – are imposing whale-backed barriers holding a series of long valleys, all 'blind' at the northern end. In one of these cwns is situated the beautiful, lonely ruin of Llanthony Abbey, whose monks deserted it as early as the 12th century. It was abandoned during the lawless reign of Stephen, yet to stand on its site and feel the mountains enclosing around, one wonders if it was not the overpowering nature of the savage scenery that overawed the brethren rather than the turmoil of marcher wars.

Middle England
Shire Country of Hedge and Pasture

One of the proudest titles attached to any area of England is 'The Shires.' This heavy, fertile land, with its flat fields and massive hedgerows, well grown elms, grazing cattle and trim farms, encompasses the counties of Middle England – notably, Leicestershire, Huntingdonshire, Staffordshire, Warwickshire, Northamptonshire and the ancient county of Rutland – their wold and fen; slow meandering rivers and gentle undulating countryside earning for the Shires the accolade of being considered the 'true' English Landscape – a homely attraction not easily paralleled in other lands, in other counties.

The enfolded fields of Middle England, their pastures enclosed by blackthorn and quick-set hedges, resemble nothing so much as a vast patchwork of landscape – a series of green meadows; golden in the aftermath of harvest; or brown, fawn and ochre where ploughed land has not yet yielded a crop. This is the traditional home of the grazier and the huntsman. The firm, sweet grass is widely spread and stock fatten on it and flourish as they do in few other places. Over these rich feeding grounds ride Britain's premier Hunts, the famous Belvoir (named from the ancestral seat of the Dukes of Rutland), the Pytchley and the Quorn. Indeed, the landscape might have been purposely laid out for hunting; even the woods seem tamed, used as fox coverts. The meads of this gently rolling clay country are punctuated by ash trees, put in as standards, and the majority of hedges date back to the Enclosure Acts of the Georgian Period when thorn was inevitably used for making a fast-growing hedgerow. They offer excellent jumping and all are wide enough to hide a fox at its last gasp.

Most of the great Hunts exult in grass, as does the dairy farmer, but where Middle England begins, so to speak, on the east, and the clay slopes rise from the peat of the Fens, the countryside, although rather heavy and flat, is first-class wheat and bean land. The latter crop has a singular association with the Midland landscape (somewhat similar to that of the hop with Kent) which makes the crimson flower of the runner bean a predominant colour in high-summer, splashing the astonishing brightness of its bloom upon both farmland, where it bines along canes, and village and hamlet where it outshines even the traditional cottage-garden flowers of stock, pansy and rose. The Northamptonshire poet John Clare held its beauties in high regard:

A Beanfield full in blossom smells as sweet
As Araby, or groves of orange flowers;
Black-eyed and white, and feathered to one's feet,
How sweet they smell in morning's dewy hours!
When seething night is left upon the flowers,
And when morn's sun shines brightly o'er the field,
The bean-bloom glitters in the gems of showers,
And sweet the fragrance which the union yields
To battered footpaths crossing o'er the fields.

As with the beauty to be found in the summer abundance of bean flowers, so is the landscape of the Shires best exemplified by the intimacy of its most common features. The true glory of England is its hedgerows, and nowhere is this more apparent than in Middle England. From the day when first commons and common-fields were enclosed, quick-hedges were planted. The slips were cut from hawthorn bushes that had always dotted the country and made breaks. These quicks set beside ditches – by reputation a yard deep and four feet across – grew like weeds and made the glorious paddocks and pastures that pattern the green mosaic that is today the surface of England. Within these hedgerows – now composed of holly, elder, hedge maple, crab apple and the ubiquitous hawthorn – are to be glimpsed the intimate treasures of the Shires.

At no other time of year are these 'glimpses' lovelier than at springtide when dripping hedgebanks and rain soaked fields are russet-brown or smokey-purple according to the play of sunlight upon the scene. The landscape is still a winter one, only flushed with spring at intervals, but birth is an imperceptible thing in nature; growth emerges quickly and suddenly in colours of misty green and grey. Its silent impetus is wonderfully evoked by Clare, writing of his native countryside:

'The dewdrops on every blade of grass are so much like silver drops that I am obliged to stoop down as I walk to see if they are pearls, and those sprinkled on the ivy-woven beds of primroses underneath the hazels, whitethorns, and maples are so like gold beads that I stooped down to feel if they were hard, but they melted from my finger. And where the dew lies on the primrose, the violet and whitethorn leaves, they are emerald and beryl, yet nothing more than the dews of the morning on the budding leaves; nay, the road grasses are covered with gold and silver beads, and the further we go the brighter they seem to

shine, like solid gold and silver. It is nothing more than the sun's light and shade upon them in the dewy morning; every thorn-point and every bramble-spear has its trembling ornament: till the wind gets a little brisker, and then all is shaken off, and all the shining jewelry passes away into a common spring morning full of budding leaves, primroses, violets, vernal speedwell, bluebell and orchis and commonplace objects.

Thus were the Shire hedgerows planted, from necessity and by law, yet they have become beautiful in themselves. The oaks, ash, sycamores and elms which form the hedge standards are perhaps the most important growths in the whole landscape of these Isles.

The North Country
Moorland, Dales and Wold

Yorkshire, Northumberland and Durham were once part of the great Saxon Kingdom of Northumbria, and these wild, often windswept counties share a history as turbulent as any in Britain. In the days before industrialism laid wide-grasping hands upon the valleys and rivers, there was scarcely a square mile of land lying between the waters of Trent and Tweed which had not some charm and beauty to reveal. But when the demand for iron-ore and coal increased as manufacturing developed, stretches of a hitherto solitary land became utterly changed in aspect and character. Fortunately the major part of the Northern landscape remains unscarred and still forms one of the largest tracts of unspoilt countryside in England.

The wolds of the East Riding, North Riding and Lincolnshire are still given over to solitude – wherein the only tenants are cattle and shaggy Swaledale sheep – and their vast distances and lonely horizons remain much as Tennyson described them,

> *'Calm and deep peace of this high wold,*
> *And on these dews that drench the furze'.*

The Peak country of Derbyshire is still an expanse of loveliness; and the great Yorkshire Dales remain unspoilt, their scattered, whitewashed farmsteads, dale villages and hamlets – a few cottages grouped together in a huddle of stunted trees, set far enough apart to give each an aspect of seclusion – are yet as Wordsworth knew them, lying deep and low at the foot of the high fells, each *'beneath its little patch of sky, and little lot of stars'.* Solitude, isolation from the world of industry, which is, after all, so near – these are still the prevalent characteristics of the northern dales and wolds.

Moorland, like mountain, is one of the permanencies of landscape, and has been called the 'last English wilderness'. Such a description is particularly worthy of the high, cold countryside of the Yorkshire moors and those of Durham and Northumberland, whose wide, open vistas and immense, birdswept skies are the hunting-ground of *'dapple-dawn-drawn'* falcons – the noble *'windhovers'* of the rolling plain. In summer,

when moorlands 'blow' with the flowers of wild eglantine and hairbells, the prevailing colour of the land is stained with the purple of heather and the yellow of vast swags of gorse and broom; yet in winter's grip – if the moors have not become interfolding acres of drifting snow and hazy blue shadow – the colour of the landscape takes on a sinister hue – reflecting the predominant granite rocks in bleak greyness, or in the browns of dead bracken. Probably the best known northern moors are those of the West Riding – at Keighley and Wadsworth – because of their nearness to the Brontë family home at Haworth. A lane near the Parsonage leads out onto the moorland, where, in the stark winter weather of 1848, Charlotte set out in search of a sprig of heather, thinking it might revive her dying sister Emily. The spirit of these wild places is sombre; leaden clouds suppress the landscape, and dry-stone walling which patterns the valleys shows grey in the sunlight, and black in rain – yet under such dark cloud the moor itself turns a deep green beneath the stillness of heather and gorse.

The Pennines stretch from Derbyshire to the farthermost parts of Northumberland and offer some of England's finest walking country. Huge expanses of upland moor – looking much as they have done since the beginning of history – sweep to a score of summits of more than 2,000 feet in the Yorkshire Dales. Over a million years ago, ice flowing down the eastward tilt of the Pennine watershed carved out the dales in their distinctive shapes. Wensleydale, watered by the River Ure, with its ravines and spectacular waterfalls of Hardraw Force and the cataracts of Aysgarth, is the broadest, most open and well-forested of the Yorkshire valleys, where tree, rock and river combine to make a prospect of rare charm. Swaledale, its sudden twists and sinuous windings beneath its steep hills, has a more secluded grandeur, and narrower, tributary dales, such as Arkengarthdale, Bishopdale and Coverdale burrow deep between the flanks of the fells. These hills are of limestone, capped here and there by millstone grit, and upon them grow cotton grass and heather, flecked with bilberry and crowberry. There is also softer natural beauty among the rugged landscape – in the treasury of Alpine flowers left behind by the Ice Age around Teesdalehead in Durham; and in the valleys are the remains of monastic buildings that are scattered all over the North East. Yorkshire's Fountains Abbey, founded in 1132, is the best known; Bolton Priory ('Abbey' as it is locally, but erroneously, called) set in a wooded gorge besides the River Wharfe; and Rievaulx Abbey, which is perhaps the most romantically sited of all.

In Northumberland the Pennines merge imperceptibly with the Cheviot Hills – its moors and dales – whose remote summits command inspiring views of the Tweed gliding away to Berwick and the far sea; and beyond the river, the smiling, placid acres of the Scottish Lowlands. Walter Scott wrote of this landscape: *The Cheviots were before me in frowning majesty; not indeed with the smiling majesty of rock and cliff which characterises mountains of the primary class, but huge round-headed and cloathed with a dark robe of russet, gaining by their extent and desolate appearance an influence upon the imagination, as a desert district possessing a character of its own'.* In the past these solitary hills were the scene of much border dispute and bloodshed, made famous in ballads such as 'Chevy Chase' which celebrates the battle between the armies of Earl Douglas and the Percys of Northumberland. These hills, which once resounded to the clash of sword and claymore in the fierce hand-to-hand fighting of the Border Wars, now echo only to the cry of the curlew. Amid the Cheviots' magnificent scenery – where star saxifrage and spring gentians are still to be found – rise the bold domes of the hills, riding across the border like massive waves.

The North West
Lakeland, Mountain and Fell

Cumbria, land of misty mountains and placid lakes, has a landscape of dramatic light and shade which possesses all the grandeur and concentrated beauty of configuration that one usually associates with the Alps. English Lakeland, with its sweeping fells and dales, is probably the most definitely bounded of all Britain's regions – lying between the massive divide of the Pennine highlands on the east and the sea-coast on the west; to the north stretches the wide spread of the Solway Firth, whilst the silver tidal-flats of Morecombe Bay denote its southern limit. In past ages the land was densely wooded, and was so remote from the rest of England that Cumbria was looked upon as a natural part of Scotland until late Norman times. The Rey stone on Stainmoor was then regarded as the boundary marker between English and Scottish thrones – as it still is the marker between Cumbria and the rest of England.

Such rugged terrain remained empty, or nearly so, until it was populated by the last of the great migrations into Britain due to the wanderings and settlements of the Vikings, which took them to Iceland, Greenland and even to the seaboard of Newfoundland; and in Britain, to the occupation of Shetland, the Orkneys, the Isle of Man and much of Western Scotland. In the 10th century they took possession of this land of purple mountains and lakes of inky-blackness, whose desolation must have appeared to them out of the mists, out of the rain, in all its ancient terror. However, the Norsemen stamped their indelible mark upon what is now called the 'Lake District' and nearly all the place names of Cumberland and Westmorland are of their tongue – 'dale' and 'fell', 'force' (a waterfall), 'thwaite' (cleared ground), and 'tarn' from the nordic word 'tiorn' (a tear). The Vikings are also responsible for the most fascinating relics of the district – the crosses of Gosforth and Bewcastle. The former displays a strange mixture of pagan myth and Christian symbolism, whilst the latter cross is incised in the tradition of Byzantine craft with a strength of design and power of execution that points to close links between their lakeside settlements and the distant Bosphorus, perhaps by the Viking trade routes to the Black Sea and Russia.

The region of high, windswept fells, rock crags and distant views of lofty, broken peaks, centres around the mountainous mass that culminates in Scafell and Scafell Pike – which at 3,210 feet is the loftiest peak in England. These are the spectacular images of Wordsworth's poetry:

'The mountains against heaven's grave weight
Rise up, and grow to wondrous height'.

Geographically the area is the domed uplift of the earth's crust, formed by volcanic activity, which has exposed the oldest and hardest rocks at its centre – from where running water has cut dales which radiate like spokes from a wheel from the mountain knot of the Scafell crests. Later, the weight of the Ice Age worked its effect upon the landscape we know today. Sheeted thick with glaciers, the slow movement of ice cut into the valley floors, and when the warmer ages came there were deeply gouged hollows and valleys – dammed by glacial debris – into which the melting waters flowed. Here the grandeur of mountains and the bold austerity of rock crags are mirrored in the still waters of the area's myriad lakes. Among the most notable of these lakes are the lovely Ennerdale Water, Buttermere, Crummock Water, Windermere and Derwent Water – each fed by the crystal streams and rivers of this, the rainiest region in England. Their surface is of an exquisite, piercing turquoise that is not a reflection of the sky, although it may be enhanced by it just as it is changed and patterned by every breath of wind. With the wild scent of bracken and the distant whisperings of waves lapping against reeds, the English Lakes possess a calm serenity. It is the secret haunt of the Lakeland spirit – a landscape of poetic intensity – of ice-blue waters that lie placid among the heights:

'Nought wakens or disturbs their tranquil tides,
Nought but the char that for the may-fly leaps,
And breaks the mirror of the circling deep.'

The most spectacular of the Lakes is also the deepest. Wast Water lies like a stretched silken cloth, scarcely wrinkled in the shadow of Great Gable and The Screes. With volcanic rock and sculptured, marble-like cliffs gathered on all sides, Wast Water comes closer than any other to the primitive state of glacial mere. Its waters are so exceptionally pure that it supports little wildlife – save for char, minnows and sticklebacks.

Lowland Scotland
The Borders and the Uplands

Traditionally, the southern half of Scotland is known as the Lowlands – a description which might suggest flatness and a certain lack of variety, yet nothing could be further from the truth. The Lowlands – a tableland of grassy hills and cool green pastures – stand in dignity, possessing a loveliness that is apt to be overlooked in comparison with the more dramatic splendours that the rugged North-western Highlands can provide. The midland valley between the Forth and the Clyde (the region's uppermost extent) is the only lowland area in the literal sense of the word; and the southern uplands rise to the Tweedsmuir Hills in the centre and the Lammermuir and Pentland Hills in the north-east. Indeed, the Scottish Lowlands are more hilly than most parts of England, and the climate, particularly in the central areas, can be as harsh in mid-winter – when the first flurries of snow come scudding over the summits – as that endured by any lonely hamlet in the Highland mountains.

As always in Scotland, the most dramatic landscapes are to be found where there are hills of size; and each has its own descriptive name: 'dods' are rounded summits; 'laws' are conical hills, and 'rigs' are ridges. Of the Lowland type, the most perfect specimens are to be found in the district where the Solway flats climb northwards over the watershed into Lanarkshire and the valley of the Clyde. These are not the fearsome hills of continual rock outcrop that give the mountains of the west and north their terrifying character, but gentle and wooded for the most part – where conifers and patches of green fields lie in the strath, ascending through skirting mists to where the grey mares' tails of mountain waterfalls send their drifts of spray among moss and rock-clinging fern.

The hills rise out of flat farming land, climbing among forests until, imperceptibly, the farmsteads become smaller, the rivers dwindle to brown streams, and growing crops give place to smooth, bronze-green hillsides, marked here and there with a fan of scree thrown out by an occasional winter torrent. Then the deciduous trees disappear and in their stead are found an occasional clump of fir or a plantation of spruce, and little burns run through deep ditches cut in the soft peat. As the air grows colder and the gradient finally eases, you can see mile upon mile of moorland, of which the feature is mainly its curious straw-brown colour, with a tarn here and there reflecting whatever colouring may be in the sky, and all the while, the cries of peesweeps and lambs emphasise the loneliness. In the far distance the landscape mingles with the ocean, and the words of Wordsworth seem to carry in the still air:

> . . . a silver current flows
> With uncontrolled meanderings;
> Nor have these eyes by greener hills
> Been soothed in all my wanderings.

Where the Lowlands run into the sea there are high cliffs and remote beaches of white sand; endless vistas of foam-flecked tides reveal at the foot of every other cleft in the sea-cliff a fine old fishing village with woods about it that might have been lifted directly from remote East Anglia or the coastline of Friesland. It may be a place as big as Eyemouth – large enough to lose a score of able-bodied men in one night of storm – or it might be small and quaint and a trifle bleak like St Abb's, perched on a promontory overlooking a harbour continually assailed by waves. It may be snug and pretty like Burnmouth, or large like Dunbar: yet these fishing communities run to type – and that a rather distinguished type – born of the constant battle between fishermen and the treacherous ocean with its fanged reefs, cross currents and sudden violent storms.

A paradox of Scotland is that these harsh coasts are backed by agricul-

tural land of a particularly rich quality. The fields run back from the edge of the cliffs to the hills, green and fruitful; the traditional white walls of the Scots farmsteads making delicious splashes against the monotone of pasture and land under plough. There are not many red roofs in Scotland; the common blue slate covers most of even the rural roofs, but their sombre gleaming above whitewash can make lovely effects against slopes that rise from the ploughed red soil, to where black-faced sheep and wild red deer crop the hard, thin grass of the upland, and where the golden eagle soars overhead.

In this peaceful landscape there are scars of a turbulent past; in the magnificent ruins of castles – Tantallon, Slains and Dunnottar – each overhanging the sea from its rocky crag; and in the gutted remains of great abbeys – Kelso, Jedburgh and Dryburgh – laid to waste by English invaders from the 13th to the 17th centuries. The English, however, were not the only despoilers, for there was dark treachery even among their own kind – notably by the Border reivers, or mosstroopers, and the powerful Border Earls. Wars and feuds, abduction and murder were commonplace, and 'cattle-lifters' raided to the very gates of Edinburgh, showing their contempt for royal authority. Yet out of these deeds come the tales of the 'makkars'— the poets and the 'makers' of ballads. Their stories of love and of war, often laced with sardonic wit, were told in broad Scots. In the hands of the makkars – as in those of Robert Burns – this deceptively harsh language can become a tool of great beauty.

The Highlands
Mountains, Lochs and Islands

The Scottish Highlands possess the most magical and yet the most terrifying landscape in Britain. Coming up country from the border, through agricultural land full of grey stone and rounded hills, dotted with vestiges of medievalism – ruined castles and bare skeletons of broken abbeys – you see the jagged frieze of the Grampians (the highest and largest mountainous mass in Britain) rise above the northern horizon, blue and dramatic and unmistakable. Their capacity – perhaps an effect of atmospherics – to take on at a distance a wistful, cerulean blue, characterizes all the great mountain ranges of the Scottish Highlands – the Monadhliaths, the Trossachs, the Cairngorms of the Central Heights, and the isolated mountains of the far north. These awesome ranges share the landscape with wild sea lochs that gouge deeply into the land; with icy streams that tumble through green and wooded glens; with frowning crags and darkly shadowed passes; with the calm waters of vast inland lochs and kyles; and, above all, with an ever changing sky that gives rise to an immense variety of shade and subtle hue.

Perhaps the almost excessive popularity of the Highlands is a lingering remnant of Victorian sentiment. It was certainly popularised in the minds of the public by Queen Victoria's affection for similar scenes of Deeside and the general acceptance of that romantic spirit so well encompassed by the nickname *'Balmorality'.* To take this combination of pretty images; of conifers, rivers and lakes as a complete representation of the Highlands is to miss beauty infinitely more austere, profound and elusive. Indeed, it does not take any Scottish byway long to rise out of its glen to the high countryside of the mountains – through woods that degenerate into clumps of birch and hazel growing on land that hardens with every hundred feet of altitude gained, until there is only bare rock and moorland scrub. It is not a comfortable scene that meets the wayfarer's eye – but one to marvel at in all its gaunt and threatening majesty. Here is a landscape which changes from green to the brown of peat moors and the silver dazzle of spasmodic torrents fashioned fantastically by the volcanic and glacial crises of the distant past. It seems a cold and lonely place, snow-laden in the dead of winter and often assailed by driving rain; yet beauty, when it is found is – perhaps in the play of cloud-shadows on the bare, bronzed slopes, or the trail of mist across the rocky face of mountains – by its unsuspected nature, all the more enchanting.

Although splendid desolation is now the motif of the Central Highlands – given over to the raven and the deer – it is as well to remember that the countryside was once the home of crofters who contrived to eke out a living from the bleak surroundings: and it is here that clansmen defended these grim passes to the point of death. At Dalwhinnie in the valley of the swift Spey the clans of old gathered in warlike array. Here they repulsed Cromwell in his day, and, more than a century later, the Hanoverian army of General Cope. Further down the glen, near Kingussie, Ruthven Barracks were built in 1718 to keep the Highlands in check, but Bonnie Prince Charlie's Jacobite rebels destroyed them in 1746. The present desolation of these uplands is largely the result of the collapse of his cause and its ultimate destruction on Culloden Moor (surely the most drear and melancholy of all Scottish battlefields). In reprisal, crofters were forcibly evicted from their farmsteads by English troops carrying out their commission against the King's enemies. Every corner of the Highlands seems to have its touching reminder of the troubles – a ruined croft or crumbling barn – recalling the savage depopulation of the 18th and 19th centuries, when the ancestral homeland of its Celtic inhabitants was 'cleared' to make room for large scale sheep farming and English Baronial estates.

The tremendous mountain masses of the Central Heights, however imposing, are at certain seasons so hostile, so acid in colour, that their wilderness depresses rather than exalts the spirit. But towards the west the softer, more poetic light of a moister, warmer climate informs scenes of picturesque splendour with a strange and irrepressible charm. Here are found the main elements – mountains, lochs and islands – in the triumphant chord of Highland beauty. A glance at the map of Scotland reveals how fresh water lochs endlessly stud the region, and how fantastically the western coastline is indented by the sea. Here, tortuous fjords add to the scenic effect, allowing the mysteries of the oceans to send their groping fingers amid the mountains, and to fumble among the tangles of golden weed that line its shores. Near at hand the water is vivid blue, paling into a white brilliance when a burst of sunlight from the sombre sky dazzles the surface, contrasting with the green of its low isles, and, in mid-summer, the yellow of cut hayfields on the far shore. Indeed, on the raw rock of mountain and on the white sands of the tideline, on pasture and on moor, the light cast by the sky and reflected by the sea plays amazing tricks of colour. In storm and in calm it combines in a thousand different ways to present to the seeing eye all the essences of Highland landscape – be it in the violet shades of distant peaks, or in the warm indigo sheen which falls upon fishing villages such as Crail, in Fife. Even Bothwell Castle in Lanarkshire has a pink wash of light at some times of day. How bathed in such light stands Iona, from where Columba started his mission and where his cathedral now abuts the western surf. Deep-cut shadows haunt the memory of Glencoe, darken the Achnashallach Forest, and fall gently across the ruins of Melrose Abbey – reputed to hold the heart of Robert the Bruce.

Sunshine and storm-shadow breathe majestically upon the North Yorkshire moors (right) where a 'green lane' winds its sinuous course through sheep pastures and upland grazing. In the Pennines, these splendid grassy tracks are called 'thrufts'. They were originally routed during the New Stone Age – 4,000 years ago – and were used extensively by stock drovers up until the mid-nineteenth century.

A harsh frost and the first flurries of light snow lend enchantment to the English landscape of late autumn. The unaccustomed brightness of winter's dawning and strange unheavenly glare call to mind the words of Thompson's verse –

'The lengthen'd Night elaps'd, the Morning shines
Serene, in all her dewy Beauty bright,
Unfolding fair the last Autumnal Day.
And now the mountain Sun dispels the Fogs;
The rigid Hoar-Frost melts before his Beam;
And hangs on every Spray, on every Blade
Of Grass, the myriad Dew-Drops twinkle round.'

Above: flower-fields of clover and buttercup in the Yorkshire Dales.

Wild poppies and corn are inseparable: the Romans depicted their corn-goddess Ceres with a lighted torch in one hand and a sheaf of poppies in the other; and even today we view the brilliant scarlet of the corn poppy and the dusty yellow of wheat as the most perfectly elemental colours of high summer. Along the field margin *right* a skein of vivid scarlet enlivens the Suffolk land-scape – its drowsy, uncompromising colour recalling Keats' words –

'. . . soft lifted by the winnowing wind;
Or on a half-reap'd furrow sound asleep,
Drows'd with the fumes of poppies, while thy hook
Spares the next swath and all its twined flowers.'

Through bare grey dell, high woods and pastoral cove;
. . . where peace to Grasmere's lonely island leads,
To willowy hedgerows, and to emerald meads;
Leads to her bridge, rude church, and cottage grounds,
Her rocky sheepwalks, and her woodlands bounds.'

Winter views from the land of Wordsworth's inspiration. Lake Grasmere in a frozen calm *facing page* with the brooding peaks of Stone Arthur and Heron Pike. Haweswater *below* is the most isolated of all the English Lakes, and Helvellyn *right* is one of the most beautiful. *Lower right and left:* the Crinkle Crags and Blowfell.

The Downland valleys of Southern England were once shrouded in dense forests; yet the early Jutish and Saxon settlers – who incised the massive chalk figure at Wilmington in Sussex *far right* – also cleared the wealden valleys of their impenetrable veil of woodland. Thus was created a broad, fertile land of green pastures and scattered wood-coppice; of lush open grasslands interspersed with enchanting villages half-hidden beneath the shade of towering elm and oak. From the heights of the Downs, the scene stretches away before the eye in almost biblical splendour – of ripening wheat, and heavily laden orchards – until it finally meets and mingles with Kipling's 'wooded, dim blue goodness of the distant horizon.'

White chalk breaks through the furrow at Lambourne Down, near Eastbury *right and below. Lower right:* plough and pastureland in Gloucestershire.

'So the lush Weald to-day
Lies green in distance, and the horizon's sweep
Deepens to blue in woods, with pointed spire
Pricking the foreground by the village tiles,
And the hop-kiln's whitened chimney stares between
Paler and darker green of Kentish miles.'

The landscape of Sackville West's poetry is one of small farms and rolling pasture, studded with villages mentioned in the Domesday Book and little changed for three or four centuries – one such hamlet is Hurstbourne Tarrant *right*. It is named from the Anglo-Saxon "Hissaburnam" – a local stream.

The ash, birch, oak and beech – the principal trees of the ancient woodlands – grow lovelier as autumn begins to encroach upon summer. It is the time of year when leaves are as gold and fire *this page* and the beech is like a beautiful eastern window in a cathedral, a 'dome of many-coloured glass', but far more varied. It has a depth as well as a pattern, and the colours change as quickly as Shelley's chameleons that 'live on light and air', awaiting the northern weather to shed the tree's thick canopy of leaf – of yellow

and black, and pale, and heretic red. Once bereft of foliage the architectural similarity is further enhanced as the sinewed trunk and branches spread forever upwards like the interwoven tracery of medieval fan-vaulting at its most intricate. Their beauteous form in winter moved Shakespeare to write –

'That time of year thou mayst in me behold
When yellow leaves, or none, or few, do hang
Upon those boughs which shake against the cold,
Bare ruin'd choirs, where late the sweet birds sang.'

In spring, however, the March winds and the early blooms of primroses, daffodils, violets and pied wind-flowers stir movement in the tree's mighty girth and subtle changes come over the tracery of the bough until the moment when they are once again ruddy with the promise of bud *right* and the flower that precedes the leaf.

'These restless surges eat away the shores
Of earth's old continents; the fertile plain
Welters in shallows, headlands crumble down,
. . . swept by the murmuring winds of ocean, join
The murmuring shores in a perpetual hymn,
. . . and gathered in the hollows. Thou dost look
On thy creation and pronounce it good.'

'Calm or convulsed . . . dark-heaving, boundless and sublime' . . . the ceaseless action of waves breaking on the Cornish headland *these pages* shows the continual interplay of fundamental forces which are gradually shaping and reshaping the precipitous cliffs of the far-western shore. The rocks are among the hardest in the country and remain as vertical, jagged pinnacles providing valuable ledges for nesting sea-birds – kittiwake, cormorant and guillemot – and the cliff-loving wild cabbage and sea campion.

Not far from St Just, the westernmost town in England, the rocky buttress of Cape Cornwall *right* confronts the sea. The actual furthest point west on the mainland of England is Land's End *above and facing page*, the famous granite mass tumbling into the sea at the end of the Penwith Peninsula.

'Old Time, though he, gentlest among the Thralls
of Destiny, upon these wounds hath laid
His lenient touches, soft as light that falls,
From the wan Moon, upon the towers and walls,
Light deepening the profoundest sleep of shade.
Relics of Kings! Wreck of forgotten wars.'

Corfe Castle in Dorset *above* assumes the imagery of a dream –
bathed and washed in the golden veil of morning mist. Here, cowled
and muted by nature, its immense solemnity and brooding presence
are further enhanced by the mysterious light and vapours of dawn.
Supreme over all – it has guarded the Isle of Purbeck since its
inception in 1086.

Right: mists roll across
the rich grazing meadows
of Hascombe in Surrey.

'Golden lie the meadows; golden run the streams;
red gold is on the pine-stems.
The Sun is coming down to earth,
and walks the fields and the waters.
The Sun is coming down to earth,
and the fields and the waters,
shout to him golden shouts.'

Meredith's words speak with the voice of English Lakeland in the heart of autumn – whose fiery tones encompass every pleasing shade of the spectrum, and blend them into countless combinations, ever changing, yet ever in perfect harmony.

The russet of moorland, the golden browns of fallen leaves, and the cerulean blue of deep lakes are the predominant hues of the Cumberland and Westmorland landscape in October and early November. The haunting solitude of Ullswater *far left, and right,* with its fine dusting of powdered snow, is encircled by the massiv domed brows of the Cumbrian Peaks. These lofty fells remain snow-covered throughout much of the year, and summits such as the Langdale Pikes *above and top left* dazzle the eye with reflected light, yet beckon forever onward to lovely, lonely places, whose solitude is broken only by the gentle murmur of a mountain stream or the occasional bleat of a moorland lamb.

'The Seasons work their will
On golden thatch and crumbling stone.'

Nowhere are John Drinkwater's words more appropriate than in the peaceful villages of the Cotswolds; their mellow, honey-coloured stone encrusted with bright lichens and the moss of centuries. A sense of timelessness sets the region apart from any other, and villages such as Castle Combe and Chipping Campden come to us today as a dream of ages past. The former *above left* – named from a Norman Castle which was once one of the strongest in the West Country – lies in a deep valley, steep sided and shaded

by tall trees. Nestling in its hollow, the twisting By Brook mirrors its three-arched medieval bridge; and a colourful group of gabled and mullioned houses lead up the hill to St Andrew's Church, which, like so many other 15th century buildings, was built through the liberality of wealthy cloth merchants. Chipping Campden *facing page* is another glory of the wolds, and to the north-east of the town lies Hidcote Manor *left* whose delightful gardens are now owned by the nation. At Compton-Wynyates in Warwickshire *above* rough-hewn stone is supplanted by Tudor brickwork. In this magnificent example of 16th century architecture the symmetry of weathered brick is further emphasised by clipped yews and hedges tailored into neat, formal shapes.

The timeless green-enchantment of the Yorkshire Dales has a particular poetic quality about its windswept terraced landscape of verdant folds and intersecting limestone walling (seen *right,* at Malham). In spring thin veins of buttercup-yellow colouring run along the land, and the sky dominated by far-off clouds that amass on distant hilltops *above.*

'. . . Nor shall the aerial Powers
Dissolve that beauty, destined to endure,
White, radiant, spotless, exquisitely pure,
Through all vicissitudes, till genial Spring,
Has filled the laughing vales with welcomed flowers'

The summer landscape of Southern England is one of rich abundance – a vast panorama o greens and gilded-yellows – a land plotted and pierced into fold, fallow and plough. At Rodney Stokes *far left* on the lower slopes of the Mendips fields of white mustard turn to gold, and the thundery heat of mid-July suppresses the canal scene at Tiverton in Devon *left* giving it a lazy, lethargic edge.

Lower left: Devon thatch, on the River Exe at Bickleigh; and *below,* the Parish Church at Madingley in Cambridgeshire unfurls its Cross of St George against a backcloth of meadow and pasture.

The chequered patchwork of delicate colouring *right*, at Harcombe is typical of the southern landscape, and is engendered by the effect of climate upon wood and field, and by the arrangement of farmsteads in gentle and unwearying composition –

'There see the clover, pea and bean
Vie in variety of green;
Fresh pastures speckled o'er with sheep;
Brown fields their fallow sabbaths keep.'

The landscape of Cumberland and Westmorland is one of grandeur, yet glimpses of tranquillity and peace – such as Aira Force near Ullswater *above* and the quiet gurgling beck of the Rothay at Ambleside *right* – infused into the Lakeland poets an affection for the area's calmer beauty which nestles beneath the bold austerity of mountain crags – their rich green vales awash with the scent of bracken and moss, and the ever present sound of bird-song.

'Not a breath of air
Ruffles the bosom of this leafy glen.
From the brook's margin, wide around, the trees
Are steadfast as the rocks; the brook itself,
Old as the hills that feed it from afar,
Doth rather deepen than disturb the calm.'

Right: Lindisfarne – famous as 'Holy Island' – has a 16th century castle perched on a mass of whinstone. *Below:* dominated by chalk cliffs which rise to a height of 600 ft, the lighthouse at Beachy Head is washed by the unpredictable waters of the English Channel.

Facing page: Mothecombe Bay in South Devon – a grey mist on the sea's face, and a grey dawn breaking – after a night of storm the waves still heave and crash with a metallic glitter encouraged by a cold wind and angry intermittent sunshine –

'The swinging waves pealed on the shore;
The saffron beach, all diamond drops
And beads of surge, prolonged the roar'.

Right: Bamburgh Castle in Northumberland, built on a basalt rock first fortified by Ida the 'Flamebearer' of Bernicia in 547 AD, and besieged by William Rufus in the 11th century. The present castle – centring on the 12th century keep – fell to Edward IV's heavy artillery in 1464.

The light of Westondale *left* has the cold, wild brightness of Yorkshire moorland. Leaden clouds suppress the landscape, and dry-stone walls pattern the dales, showing grey in sunshine and black in rain; yet under such dark cloud the moor itself is enriched – turning a deep green beneath the stillness of its birdswept skies.

The River Amble *right* cuts its sinuous course through the 'levels' north of Wadebridge, whose very flatness is reminiscent of Romney Marsh and brings to mind Tennyson's description '. . . like emblems of infinity, the trench waters run from sky to sky.'

Above: the most conspicuous man-made feature of Wasdale is the gleaming network of dry-stone walls in which the landscape around Great Gable is enmeshed. They date for the most part from the 18th century Enclosure Acts.
Right: the narrow gorge of Symond's Yat in the shire of Hereford.

'Right against the Eastern gate,
Where the great Sun begins his state,
Rob'd in flames, and Amber light,
The clouds in thousand Liveries dight'.

Here, photography captures the imagery of
John Milton's poetry, as the 'Risen Orb
of Dawn' bathes a frost-riven landscape in
its gentle iridescent glow.

The ruin of Hadrian's Wall forms the most spectacular relic of Roman Britain. The mighty wall runs across the width of northern England for 73 miles, from Wallsend to Bowness-on-Solway, and marked the north-west limit of Imperial conquest. The great square stones of Empire seem to mirror the spirit of the vast open landscape through which it sweeps over the craggy spine of Britain, punctuated by the ruins of milecastles *lower right,* turrets and forts – paralleled by steep ramparts and ditches *below* making attack from the Scottish side extremely hazardous: indeed, it was

an aspect which caused the 17th century historian William Camden to comment, 'verily I have seene the tract of it over the high pitches and steepe descents, wonderfully rising and falling'.

Above right: a sentry's eye view of the undulating central section of Hadrian's Wall, looking eastwards to the important fort of Housesteads. As with the great Northern Wall, so it is also with the Perpendicular tower of St Andrew's at Naunton *facing page* – where local stone has been so utilized and weathered that it has become an integrated feature of the landscape.

'Season of mists and mellow fruitfulness,
    Close bosom-friend of the maturing sun.'

Keats' lines are a familiar anthem to autumn – heralding what is perhaps the most visually spectacular of all the seasons. In the moment of their dying, leaves are at their most glorious, shedding their newly found tincture upon the countryside, and transforming it with the colours of beech and cherry, of spindle and thorn – each encompassing all the fiery hues that one could expect to find, even in the boldest of Fenland sunsets.

'Pleasant shall be thy way where meekly bows
    The shutting flower, and darkling waters pass,
    And where the o'ershadowing branches sweep the grass.'

Facing page: autumn tints at Parham Park in West Sussex.

There is no county in England that is without a country mansion of either beauty or of interest, and usually of both – from Vanbrugh's wild and formidable Palladian Seaton Delaval in the far north of Northumberland to Sir John Soane's calm and decorous Gothic Port Eliot in Cornwall. But the great houses are thickest upon the ground in the triangle of land encompassed by Yorkshire, Derbyshire and Warwickshire (an excellent example being the 17th century Wootton Hall, *seen right*) in a belt of country curiously mixed with moorlands and crags, pastures, mines and industry. Thus, in communities such as Bainbridge in Wensleydale *facing page* it is possible to see the history of English visual taste set out amid the history of her economic fortunes and the full variety of England's scenery.

Domestic, industrial and educational – these are but three factors for the erection of three very distinctive architectural styles – from the simplicity of local cob and thatch seen at Sapiston in Suffolk *top right;* to the purely functional constraints exhibited by the mill on the River Lathkill *above* at Alport; and the soaring aspiration of Henry VI's Gothic masterpiece of King's College Chapel, Cambridge *right*.

'Cold jewel of Winter loveliness' – the blacken lines of dry-stone walling run along the sweeping fells and dales of Troutbeck Park in Cumbria *above* to 'guard like a shepherd King their herded ands' Derwent Water *right* also stands endowed with winter

serenity, presenting an aspect of grey, ice-capped mountains and a lake of inky-blackness – where shadows fall on wings of silence, and naught disturbs the calm save for the distant whisperings of waves lapping among the brittle-dry reed-beds

One of the true glories of the English countryside are the mottled, purple bells of the snakeshead fritillary *below* which hang their heads among the spring flowers and grasses of old meadows. Since the turn of the century the plants have become increasingly rare, yet on established sites such as the damp meads of Cricklade in Wiltshire, where the Lammas land has an unbroken history of hay-growing and common grazing going back eight hundred years, they continue to flourish – bowing their sultry, chequered blooms, patched with purple, pale and dark, to the breezes of May and early June.

Below: the remote scarp o Downland presents a visior of ever-changing light

'Ye headlong torrents, rapid and profound,
Ye softer flood along the vale; and thou
A secret world of wonders in thyself?'

Glimpses of the churning waters of Tarn Beck *above* and the

Dolmens, menhirs, cromlechs, megaliths – these are the names given to the huge standing stones which loom up in the misty landscape of Britain. An air of mystery broods over their time-encrusted forms which stand cracked, tilted and stained by four thousand years of wind, snow, rain and hail.

Examples of standing stones a to be found throughout these Isles – notable examples being the henge of Keswick Carles, Cumberland *above left;* at the 'Druids Temple' near Wensleydale in Yorkshire *lowe left;* and at the Avebury stone circle *right* whose outer ring of sarsens measures a staggering 1,350 ft in diameter, and encircles the whole village. Th finest example, however, is located further south at Stonehenge *above* on windswe Salisbury Plain . . . was this mysterious circle a temple of sun? A magical shrine? An observatory for studying the heavens? Or, as has been suggested, a gigantic compute built centuries before the Greeks mastered mathematics – The colossal stones guard their secret for eternity!

Left: Bowerman's Nose on Dartmoor – not of human intent, but formed by

'Between the water and a winding slope
Of copse and thicket, leaves the eastern shore
Of Grasmere safe in its own privacy:
. . . one calm September morning, ere the mist
Had altogether yielded to the sun.'

Lakeland – filled with the soul of her poets – is a landscape where the atmosphere paints its own unique images upon the scene: be it the gilded radiance of an autumn day at Ullswater *left* or the strangely sinister effect of low-lying mists which steal into the tranquillity of Lake Grasmere *above* to shroud its calm surface in a gossamer of silver.

The English countryside in the full freshness of the awakening season. Here, spring veils woodland and coppice margins in budding flower and verdant burgeoning leaf. Nowhere is the season's richness more apparent than in the yearly abundance of bluebells *right* – shifting and lapping in the breeze – which impart upon the woods of late April and May a sparkled, submerged glow, like light reflected and scattered from water.

The poet John Clare wrote of the uncompromising way the flowers drench the ground –

'Bluebells, how beautiful and bright they look,
Bowed o'er green moss and pearled in morning dew,
Shedding a shower of pearls as soon as shook:
In every wood-hedge gap they're shining through,
Smelling of spring and beautifully blue.'

It is the archaean setting of low, habitable dale, counterpoised against the force and magnitude of mountain scenery which gives the north-western landscape – and Lakeland in particular *this page* – its 'romantic' appeal. In the early 19th century the area's 'picturesque and romantic' image drew Wordsworth, Keats and Shelley to the English Lakes. They were, in fact, following in the footsteps of Thomas Grey, who had found 'this little unsuspected paradise' forty years before William and Dorothy Wordsworth immortalized the Lake District in prose and verse. On his original 'discovery' of Grasmere *lower left* Grey gives us this enchanting insight into his vision of the Cumbrian scene – 'The bosom of the mountains spreads here into a broad basin, discovered in the midst of Grasmere Waters; its margin is hollowed into small bays, with eminences, some of rock, some of the soft turf, that half conceal and vary the figure of the little lake they command . . . hanging enclosures, cornfields and meadows as green as emerald, with their trees and hedges and cattle, fill up the whole space from the edge of the water, and a small lawn, embosomed in old woods which climb halfway up the mountainsides and discover, above, a broken line of crags that crown the scene.'

The sloping fells of Lake Buttermere *above right* show as a dark stain reflected in its water. *Above left:* Tarn Hows, Cumbria.

Facing page: autumn at Burnham Beeches in Buckinghamshire, whose tranquil beauty is very much one of 'flash and shadow.'

The serrated coastline of the Isle of Purbeck *above and right* has always been regarded as typically English, and it is from the southern chalk cliffs (whose erosion by the North Sea separated the British Isles from the continent) that Britain derives its ancient name and proudest epithet – 'Albion'. The luminous chalk seems to saturate the air with its brilliance, bleaching even the colour of the sky and the green of the springy turf and the wild thyme on the cliff tops – creating an atmosphere and sparkle found nowhere else.

'where creeping Waters ooze,
Where Marshes stagnate, and where Rivers wind,
Clusters the rolling Fogs, and swim along
The dusky-mantled Lawn'.

Right: the March sun has gone down, and as the
evening air begins to cool a mist forms over a
sheltered Hampshire pond.

'I saw old Autumn in the misty morn
Stand shadowless like Silence, listening
To silence'.   THOMAS HOOD

A Surrey landscape *right* where thin veils of mist
wash among sheltering bands of hedgerow trees
and woodland copse, forming 'islands' in a sea of
vapour – until all is lost to the distant horizon.

Softly emerging from a white
gossamer of mist the chill
winter landscape *these pages* is
encrusted with frost, and every
tree branch and bracken frond
is loaded with twinkling hoar-
crystals. Even a barbed-wire
fence is patterned with beauty –
fringed generously with
diamonds set in silver – and the
driest, dullest bents or decayed
seed-heads of kex, or thistle, or
mugwort become as fair as
spring flowers.

'What time the blue mist round the patient cows
Dim rises from the grass and half conceals
Their dappled hides . . .'   JOHN CLARE

Right: a pale sun has risen to scatter the morning's mist, and coldly
dawns upon the frost-bitten landscape where winter's grip has
deepened the solitude and repose of the scene.

Far left: a tractor upturns a
furrow, and screaming seagulls
(which invariably follow the
winter plough) drop to the
upturned rut to feast upon the
uncovered wealth of mealy-
worms and leather-jackets. A
month later, in early April, both
lambs and cherry blossom are
well established. New-mown hay
is reaped during late May *top
right* to be retained as fodder for
winter stock *above.*

'A firmament of purple light
Which in the dark earth lay,
More boundless than the depth of night
And purer than the day.'
PERCY BYSSHE SHELLEY

The fire of a molten sun in an icy-sky infuses the winter landscape *this page* with dusky, tawny gradations of luminous colour in the wake of its setting; and for a moment in time the barren land is silhouetted against the golden horizon and capricious purple heavens.

Built in the dawn of history, the pagan cathedral of Stonehenge *right* was a Celtic shrine whose fame extended even as far as ancient Crete. Although we know it was constructed over a period of five centuries – from 1900 BC until 1400 BC – the motives that inspired this great engineering feat, unique in prehistoric Europe, are unknown. However, at least two factors indicate that worship was directed towards the heavens: the entrance to the temple is aligned to the solstice sunrise, and golden sun-discs have been uncovered during archeological excavations.

Closely packed cottages align the quayside of Bosham harbour *above* with the Saxon tower of Holy Trinity Church rising above them. When the tide-waters retreat, oystercatchers, gulls and wildfowl settle along the irregular shoreline. The tiny West Sussex village claims to be the site where Canute commanded the sea to turn back.

The medieval gem of Leeds Castle in Kent *right* is built upon an island set romantically in the reflected waters of its encircling moat. The majestic stronghold was raised in 1120, and served as both the home of Henry VIII's first wife, Catherine of Aragon, and as the prison of his daughter, Elizabeth, before she became queen.

Dorset, with its heathland and clustered hamlets of thatched cottages (such as Swan Green, *right* and *facing page*) is Thomas Hardy country. He knew Shaftsbury and its steep, cobbled Gold Hill *below* – featuring the town in his novels under its ancient name 'Shaston'.

Like a wandering Midas, the golden hand of autumn emblazens all it touches – be it an overshadowed lane of beech and oak *far right,* or the evening's reflection upon the shallow hunting grounds of coot and hern *lower right.*

Winter mists and frost create a strangely silent world of mystery, where rime has delicately spun its crystal thread spider-like, from point to point, to tracery the trees and diamond-broidery their barren branches. They sparkle with the lifting and vanishing mist *left, and above left* **to reveal a land of unaccustomed brightness and unheavenly glare – a world of stillness, of silence, and myriad points of trembling light** *above right.*

'. . . The cherished fields
Put on their winter robe of purest white.
'Tis brightness all; save where the new snow melts
Along the mazy current. Low the woods
Bow their hoar head; and ere the languid sun
Faint from the west emits his evening ray,
Earth's universal face, deep hid and chill.'

'I see the waves upon the shore,
Like light dissolved in
    star-showers, thrown'.
SHELLEY

The cold green swell of the Atlantic ceaselessly breaks against the Cornish headland at St Ives *right*. These 'mighty waters rolling' shower-forth their jewels of spray to reflect the sapphirine sky, the white breasts of gulls and the darting flight of the sandpiper.

Left: at Seaford Head in East Sussex the dazzling chalk of the South Downs abut the sea with precipitous cliffs that rise sheer-face above the tideline. In Dorset, erosion has formed distinctive scallop-shaped bays at Stair Hole, Lulworth Cove *below left* and at Man O'War Bay *below.* Upon the encircling heights dense cushions of pink-flowered thrift flourish, and sea purslane and golden samphire take root.

'Away! the moor is dark beneath the moon,
Rapid clouds have drank the last pale beam of even:
Away! the gathering winds will call the darkness soon,
And profoundest midnight shroud the serene lights of heaven.'
PERCY BYSSHE SHELLEY

The moon has risen, and its broken, trembling light shines through the mottled cloud of night, to cast earthly objects into silhouettes of strange and magnificent depth. Horsey Mill on the Norfolk Broads *far right* and the Life Boat Station at Selsey *lower right* are viewed afresh; yet the most impressive recipients of the night are those great monuments raised by peoples long-lost to history – whose premier shrine at Stonehenge *right* may now be seen in all its dramatic relation to the rolling expanse of its downland setting with an unalloyed feeling of awe and elation. Like most of the medieval cathedrals, this most celebrated of prehistoric sanctuaries was built over several periods and altered and enlarged according to changing ideas and aspirations.

Durham Cathedral *right* set on its lofty outcrop of sandstone above the valley of the Wear, wonderfully encourages that sense of continuity which is man's surest support in the face of his own mortality.

Ragged layers of evening cloud foregather upon the distant crags of the Cader Idris range near Dolgellau *above* and the chill winter's air encourages trails of mist to skirt the cwms: recalling Clare's verse –

'This twilight seems a veil of gauze and mist
Trees seem dark hills between the earth and sky
Winds sob awake and then a gusty hist
Fans through the bracken like serpents gliding by'.

The white-water of the rapid River Dee *right* at Llangollen.

Caernarvonshire is a region of rugged eminence, and from its centre rises the mountainous mass of Snowdon. Its shapely peak foreshadows those of its neighbours *above* to look down upon their deep rock-girt cwms bejewelled with gleaming tarn, or 'llyns', and narrow passes

bounded by soaring heights – strewn with boulders from the crags. One such vale is the Pass of Llanberis *right* flanked by the mighty buttress of the Snowdonia Heights – a land where the ancient spirit of Welsh freedom seems never to have been conquered –

'Eryri! temple of the bard!
And fortress of the free!
'Midst rocks which heroes died to guard
Their spirit dwells with thee!'

FELICIA HEMANS

'Beautiful must be the mountains whence ye come,
And bright in the fruitful valleys the streams,
wherefrom Ye learn your song:

The poetry of Bridges captures something of the magical quality of the infant Conway as it meanders downstream from its source in a lonely mountain llyn. At the Falls of Conway the river is swollen by the Machno, and combined waters take a headlong course down a narrow gorge *below* fringed with swaying birches and shaded with alder, oak and ash. Then through the exquisite Fairy Glen *left* by many a silver cascade and many a rock-bound pool, the river hastens to lower levels where it joins the Lledr.

The River Wye sweeps and turns through the Forest of Dean and near Symond's Yat forms a spectacular, almost complete loop *above*. The different geological strata of Carboniferous Limestone, Coal and Old Red Sandstone are crossed several times and these differences are reflected in the dense woodlands that cloak much of the valley sides – their deep shade attracting pied flycatchers and wood warblers; polecat, fallow deer and otter. *Right:* down attractive vales, which autumn has touched with loveliness, runs a lane near Betws-y-coed – bounded by the wooded heights of the Gwydwr Forest, above which rise loftier hills reaching to the distant Carnedds.

'The Orkney Islands, mountains, capes, and heights,
And lengthened stretch of bay-indented coast,
Whose cliffs arise, a bold, defiant host,
From which the shattered might of ocean reels.'
GRANT

Assailed and battered by foam-flecked Atlantic breakers, the sea-cliffs of Scotland's West Coast and Orkney Isles *these pages* are among the most spectacular in the world. The whole scene is drenched by salt-spray and drowned in the continual pounding thunder of waves and the constant wail of screaming sea-birds.

In the Highlands of Scotland one is always aware of the mountains – their breathtaking grandeur rising above the lochs and tiny crofts – Glencoe in Argyllshire, and Ben Nevis (seen *above*, from Banavie) the highest mountain in the British Isles. The historian Macaulay described the former, the Pass of Glencoe *right*, as 'the most melancholy of all the Scottish passes – the

very Valley of the Shadow of Death' – he was of course referring to the massacre of 1692, when a company of soldiers under a Campbell commander murdered more than forty McDonalds who had received them hospitably for twelve days – the memory of which taints the region with the air of treachery and infamy to this day.

The most magical and yet the most terrifying scenery in the British Isles – the Highlands of Scotland – are a land of awesome mountain ranges and wild sea lochs, of frowning crags and darkly shadowed passes, whose grandeur moved Scott to write of it '. . . a scene of natural beauty and romance; high hills, rocks and banks waving with natural forests of birch and oak, as their leaves rustle to the wind and twinkle in the sun, gave to the depth of solitude a sort of life and vivacity.'

Remote and magnificently desolate stand the Heights of Scotland, whose torturous snow-capped summits are brought into perfect harmony, reflected in the blue waters of their lakes. Such visions are the hills of Black Mount on Rennoch Moor *above*, Loch Garry *left*, Loch Leven at Ballachullish *top left* and the River Beathach at Glen Orchy *right*, whose –

'. . . wild solitudes, lengthen'd and deep,
where the sheep's bleat or that rare sound,
the harsh scream of an eagle,
serves only to intensify the silence following after.'

Dark, moisture-laden clouds suppress the heights of Glencoe, whilst areas of blue sky and sunshine accentuate the contrast between the tremendous primeval energy of the coldly gleaming torrent and the striking irregularity of the terraces over which the great cascade of peat-coloured waters of the River Coe *left* come hurtling down. On either side of the strath rise mountains which have a singular, dark beauty all their own – composed of rocks thousands of millions of years old, and called 'metamorphic' because in the course of their torturous history they have been violently changed by heat and pressure.

Above: Eilean Donnan Castle, on its island promontory, overlooking the steel-grey waters of Loch Duich.

'Hill-tops like hot iron glitter bright in the sun,
And the rivers we're eying burn to gold as they run;
Burning hot is the ground, liquid gold is the air;
Whoever looks round sees Eternity there.'

The burnished gold of sunset reflects upon Loch Garry *above;* Loch Creran in Argyllshire *right* and Glenfinnan at the head of Loch Sheil *left*. The latter's sense of timelessness, and depth of history associated with the area, is heightened by the statue of Prince Charlie, commemorating the raising of the Jacobite Standard on the spot in 1745. Indeed, there is always a sough of the 'forty-five' among the pines and larches at Glenfinnan, and a sob and a heartache in the wind whispering through them. Here the scent of resinous fir needles mingles with that of bog-myrtle, and no-one comes by this monument without seeing in their mind's eye the galleys of the Highland clans sailing up Loch Sheil to the mustering ground of 1745.

The herring port of Mallaig *above* on the rocky shore of North Morar is
the western end of the balladeer's 'Road to the Isles', and its neighbouring
waters are among the deepest and darkest in Britain. Loch Morar, a few
miles south, is more than 1,000 ft deep and is said to possess a monster
which appears whenever a death is imminent in the clan MacDonald

The Caledonian Canal (seen *right*, at Corpach) is a magnificent relic of
19th-century engineering, which took 44 years to complete, and when it was opened
in 1847 was regarded as a wonder of the age – providing sheltered passage
between the Irish and North Seas. The canal runs the length of the fissure of the
Great Glen, and is an impressive monument to Telford, its designer

The Orkneys – remote isles of treeless moor and rugged cliffs (*below*, at Cruden Bay) – have a long history of settlement which predate their medieval ownership by Denmark, Norway and – since 1496 – Scotland, by thousands of years. Excavations have revealed dwellings used by a Neolithic people who were the contemporaries of the builders of the Stone Age monuments in Southern England – the most notable of which have come to light at Skara Brae *lower left and right*, a site once engulfed in a sea of sand, but then uncovered afresh by a storm. Brochs dating from the Pictish Era have also been excavated at Gurness Earthworks *opposite page*.

The famous Cross of Lorraine *above* on Lyle Hill, Greenock was erected to honour those Free French who died in the Atlantic. *Right:* amid a wild landscape – the haunt of wildcats and badgers, crossbills, sparrow hawks and golden eagles – stands the ruined husk of Kilchurn Castle, romantically

sited on a spit of land jutting into Loch Awe. Kilchurn Castle moved Wordsworth to write of it – 'Child of loud-throated War! the mountain-stream roars in thy hearing; but thy hour of rest is come, and thou art silent in thy ...

From the placid waters of a lake run the bracken and heath covered slopes of the Glencoe massif *right*, rising into the wave-like mountainous buttress originally hewn by ice, and now shining under a light scattering of snow. Its form recalls to mind Stephenson's words '... where the old red hills are bird-enchanted, and the low green meadows bright with sward'.

Ragged layers of cinereous cloud hang over the grey water of Loch Achnacarry *left*, and dark shadows fall upon the heights of Ben Lui *below left* by the little village of Tyndrum. On the shore of Loch Fyne is Inverary Castle *below*, the heraldic seat of the Dukes of Argyll, and the headquarters of the clan Campbell since the early 15th century.

Glenfinnan, a magnificent site at the entrance to three glens, was chosen as the mustering ground of the clans during the 1745 Jacobite rising. The Camerons and the MacDonalds gathered to the standard, as did some Stewarts and Rob Roy's MacGregors. Here – where now stands the clan memorial *above* – James was proclaimed King of Great Britain and Ireland, and his commission was read out appointing 'our dearest son Charles, Prince of Wales, to be our sole regent in our Kingdoms'. After much glory, much mismanagement, and with success almost achieved, the campaign eventually foundered in disaster at Culloden moor. Inverlochy Castle *left*, beneath the intimidating shadow of Ben Nevis, retains the ancient name of the nearby town rechristened 'Fort William' after the first Scottish rising of 1715.

The water-meads of Scotland,
half-veiled in sun-shot mist;
Renfrewshire *facing page*.

If the building of fortified tower-houses bears a direct relationship
to the prevailing level of violence and disorder then there is no
better breeding ground than the medieval realm of Scotland. The
wealth of such castles (Eilean Donnan and Castle Stalker on Loch
Laich, *below and below right,* being prime examples) is evident
throughout the land; and bears silent witness to the remark made
in 1498 by Don Pedro de Ayala that 'the Scots spend all their time
in wars, and when there is no war they fight one another.' These
bastions are quiet places now, that seem to belong to their past,
half asleep in the shadows of their castle keeps.

Eilean Donnan castle *above right,* built on a tiny, rocky island by
Alexander II in 1220 to combat Viking raiders, was bombarded into
submission by the English warship 'Worcester' during the Jacobite
rebellion when it was occupied by Spanish mercenaries. The castle
was later rebuilt from rubble by clan MacRae.

Wide flush the fields; the softening air is balm;
Echo the mountain round; the forest smiles . . .
Where, o'er the rock, the scarcely waving pine
Fills the brown shade with a religious awe'

Silver birch and oaks – mellowing to the pale gold of
autumn – lie in the strath *right* and are highlighted
against the dark shadow of conifer forests as the
ascending land gains the brae of Balquhidder

Above: a highland pasture
wrested from the forest

Nature has wrought scenery of unparalleled spectacle in the Highlands, yet lying within this wild region are glimpses of a landscape of milder shade: for here, among the airy ridges and leaping torrents, are rolling sheep pastures *lower right* set here and there with lonely tarns, or trenched with shallow burns. Here also are found deer forests embracing both woods and high grazing for cattle and horses (as seen at Strath Mashie, *right*). For winter feeding hay is harvested, and the crop is usually gathered by machine *lower left,* but the further north one travels, the more the likelihood that traditional methods of hand gathering into stooks prevail. The crofters at Colla Firth *above left* use just such a method – erecting conical haystacks for drying – a practice that has been handed down throughout the centuries.

The delicate woodland flower, the Star of Bethlehem *above,* braves the cold of April and May to open its wan, milk-white petals amid the rank growth of ivy and fern.

Evening by the shoreline of Loch Eil *above* wherein the pale
gold and grey of the sky finds faithful echo in the unstirred
waters of the 'linn'. As the light fails, a ghostly mist rises
from the heart of the silent lake. At Whiteness Voe *right*

colour is fast fading from the landscape, soon to be engulfed
in a monochromatic infinity. The limitless, enigmatic character
of this land of sea, loch and mountain, beneath a vast open sky, is
most potent, most poignant, in the pause of the hour after dusk.

Raised within settings of unequalled splendour, the ancient castles of the Highlands guard the routeways of gleaming loch and fern-rusted glen. Eilean Donnan *below, left and bottom left* stands sentinel at the strategic confluence of Lochs Duich, Alsh and Long; whilst Urquhart Castle *facing page and bottom right* rises 50 ft above the monster-haunted waters of Loch Ness, to control movement along the Great Glen – the pass out of the Western Highlands along which clan MacDonald, the Lords of the Isles, travelled in

search of plunder. Thus was raised (upon the site of a Norman motte, and an even earlier Iron Age hillfort) a 13th century stone castle, built 'for a defence against the attacks of robbers and malefactors'.

Fishing boats and pleasure steamers are the main users of the lochs and waterways; and it is here – where mountains slope down to the lakeside margins – that the awesome majesty of Highland scenery may at times be 'softened' by the occasional glimpse of a cottage or croft. The paddle steamer 'Waverley' *bottom left* is viewed in the Kyles of Bute; and yachts are at anchor on Loch Leven *left* and on the Crinan canal *bottom* which connects Loch Fyne and the Firth of Clyde with the Western Isles. Further north, at Fort William, the 500 million year old granite mass of Ben Nevis reflects in the chill waters of Loch Linnhe *below*.

Ranged along the sheltered inlet of Loch Carron is the fishing hamlet of Plockton *facing page*, flanked on the north by the Applecross mountains, which appear to rise like spectres from the turquoise calm of Loch Torridon. *Overleaf:* Kinnoull Hill, the rocky buttress of the River Tay.